JANE
GRIGSON

PUDDINGS

PENGUIN BOOKS

PENGUIN BOOKS

Published by the Penguin Group. Penguin Books Ltd, 27 Wrights Lane, London
W8 5TZ, England. Penguin Books USA Inc., 375 Hudson Street, New York,
New York 10014, USA. Penguin Books Australia Ltd, Ringwood, Victoria, Australia.
Penguin Books Canada Ltd, 10 Alcorn Avenue, Toronto, Ontario, Canada M4V 3B2.
Penguin Books (NZ) Ltd, 182 – 190 Wairau Road, Auckland 10, New Zealand · Penguin
Books Ltd, Registered Offices: Harmondsworth, Middlesex, England · These
recipes are from the following works by Jane Grigson: *English Food*, published in
Penguin Books 1977; *Food with the Famous*, first published by Michael Joseph 1979
and in Penguin Books 1981; *Good Things*, first published by Michael Joseph 1971
and in Penguin Books 1973; *Jane Grigson's Fruit Book*, first published by Michael
Joseph 1982 and in Penguin Books 1983; *The Observer Guide to European Cookery*,
first published by Michael Joseph 1984. This edition published 1996 · Copyright ©
Jane Grigson, 1971, 1974, 1979, 1982, 1984. All rights reserved · Typeset by Rowland
Phototypesetting Ltd, Bury St Edmunds, Suffolk. Printed in England by Clays
Ltd, St Ives plc · Except in the United States of America, this book is sold subject
to the condition that it shall not, by way of trade or otherwise, be lent, re-sold,
hired out, or otherwise circulated without the publisher's prior consent in any
form of binding or cover other than that in which it is published and without a
similar condition including this condition being imposed on the subsequent
purchaser · 10 9 8 7 6 5 4 3

CONTENTS

I grew up in a town devoid of fruit. There were of course apples, oranges and bananas in the shops, and one or two friends had kitchen gardens, but fruit trees were not part of our lives. There was nothing to raid when summer came along. The few blackberries were dry and sooty.

This, I imagine, is why certain experiences of fruit in my childhood remain bright, an orchard in Gloucester where old trees bent into tunnels and tresses of plums, a huge basket of strawberries that an uncle produced one day when we were visiting him in Worcestershire, raspberry canes blobbed with red and yellow fruit that met over our heads in a Westmorland cottage garden, unending peaches and water-melons of a student summer in Florence.

This special feeling towards fruit, its glory and abundance, is, I would say, universal. We have to bear the burden of it being good for us – though I would not think many people in man's history agreed with one sixteenth-century doctor who said that fruit should not be eaten for pleasure, but because it did us good. An apple a day, an orange a day have not spoilt our feelings. We respond to strawberry fields or cherry orchards with a delight that a cabbage patch or even an elegant vegetable garden cannot provoke.

As with vegetables, what moved me about fruit was the centuries of patient work that have built up the repertoire of apple, pear and strawberry varieties, that have developed cherries, peaches, plums and citrus fruit for different tastes and places. Before farming began, people cleared space round certain trees so that their fruit could grow in better light with less competition. Later soldiers, travellers and explorers brought new fruit, or better versions of familiar fruit, home with them. The excitement of the Renaissance extended to gardening too, which is something that historians leave out of their accounts. Northern gardeners took from Italy the idea of planting apricots, peaches and so on against walls so that they might benefit from the stored warmth of the bricks and stones, and the espalier method of growing fruit trees was developed particularly in France. Such methods extended the range of fruit-growing. 'No longer do we have to travel down to Touraine for a Bon Chrétien pear,' wrote one enthusiastic Parisian – pears from Burgundy and Anjou as well were being grown on the outskirts of Paris, and sold in abundance in the markets.

It was in Paris that I discovered what had moved the skilful gardeners of that period. Not just the pleasure of the fruit or the triumph of intelligence, but a grand design. I was in the Bibliothèque Nationale reading room at the end of a long day. Knowing it would be several months before we'd be back in France, I had crashed through a pile of

French books without moving from the chair. Twenty minutes was left for one English book, John Evelyn's *Complete Gard'ner*, of 1693, his translation of a book by Jean de la Quintinie, one of Europe's great gardeners, expert on melon cultivation and the conduct of orangeries. He had made the gardens at Versailles from mounds of rubble, and was in charge of all Louis XIV's other gardens. No sinecure, as Louis had a passion for fruit and vegetables and inspected their progress regularly.

I opened the book in a tired blur, started at the beginning with resignation – and suddenly woke up. Here were these two voices speaking about what had moved them to their labours, de la Quintinie producing fruit with the least faults for 'the man who has most merits' – i.e., the Sun King – and Evelyn trying to turn Britain into an Elysian parkland, dotted with fine gardens. To explain what they were about, they chose fruit – 'Fruit, as it was our primitive, and most excellent as well as most innocent food, whilst it grew in Paradise; a climate so benign, and a soil so richly impregnated with all that the influence of Heaven could communicate to it; so it has still preserved, and retained no small tincture of its original and celestial virtue.' Even in its fallen state, fruit is still the most 'agreeable closure' to a meal, however grand and princely. And so it is the gardener's labour 'to repair what the choicest and most delicious fruit has been despoiled of, since it grew in Paradise'. To aim, in other words, at recovering the original flavour of Eden,   3 even if such transcendent perfection can never quite be achieved.

I suppose we no longer believe that God Almighty first planted a garden. Heavy cropping seems to be the aim of fruit breeders today, rather than fine quality of flavour. For this reason I am grateful to have been able to live and work part of my life in France during the last twenty years, in one of the great fruit-growing areas. In that genial climate, in private gardens at least, it is possible to sense what Evelyn and de la Quintinie and their tribe were after. People in Kent and Herefordshire, in Gloucestershire, Evesham and the Carse of Gowrie, may sometimes have a chance to sense it, too – so will people who stop by the occasional box of perfect fruit, nectarines perhaps or muscat grapes, on a market stall or in a supermarket, if they are not in too much of a hurry.

[*Fruit Book*]

BUTTERED APPLES

Pommes au Beurre

Only after the great public holiday of 15 August, the Assumption of the Virgin, do you begin to notice the apple trees showing their fruit. At least in the Val du Loir on the northern edge of Touraine. At market the following week, the first red and yellow reinette apples from neighbouring Anjou are on sale. Like our Cox's or Blenheims, they are ideal for this family pudding that I have never come across outside France. To me, it is perfect cooking, what food at home should always be like. Good ingredients treated simply and with affection.

My one concession to culinary art is to clarify the butter before I start cooking, by boiling it up in a small pan and then tipping it through a lined sieve into the sauté pan I use for the apples. If the butter goes in straight from the packet, something happens to make me turn my back on the stove – cats, children, telephone – and the apples burn. With clarified butter, you have some leeway, as its catching point is higher.

Peel, core and cut into eight wedges one apple for each person. Sprinkle with lemon or orange juice, or drop straight into lightly salted water. Drain and dry before frying.

Cook the slices gently in one layer – two batches, or two pans may be needed – in a wide sauté or frying pan. When the undersides cook to an autumn brown, turn the slices over and sprinkle the pan with 2 generous tablespoons of caster sugar. It soon begins to caramelize. Watch the pan carefully. Sprinkle the apples with a little cinnamon if you like.

Put the slices on a serving dish. Deglaze the pan with water or cider or apple juice; if a glass of Calvados can go in as well, so much the better. Keep stirring. Pour in some cream – single, whipping or double – to make a little sauce, 5 and add a knob of butter to freshen the buttery flavour. Spoon over the apples and serve.

[*Fruit Book*]

APPLE DUMPLINGS FROM ANJOU

SERVES 6

Upside-down apple dumplings are made in Anjou with the local variety, the reinette du Mans. You will not find it in this country. Use other firm aromatic eating apples instead. Or look out for Ribston pippins which were first grown, it is said, from reinette pips brought from Normandy in 1709. The original tree at Ribston Hall, Knaresborough, lasted for over a hundred years. A shoot from it grew into a tree that was blown over for good and all in 1928.

Make a plain shortcrust pastry with 500 g (1 lb) of flour, butter and lard. You can use a sweet pastry if you prefer it, but I find the plain kind best for fruit pies and dumplings. Form the dough into a roll, and rest it in the refrigerator for at least half an hour.

Peel and core the apples; stuff the cavities with butter and sugar mashed together, or with jam – Elizabeth David suggests plum or quince – which can be given a little extra fire by a judicious spoonful of brandy or other appropriate alcohol.

Place each apple on a square of pastry. Draw up the points and fasten them together on top. Press the edges together as well. You can put a neat circle of moistened pastry over the points, if you like. Make a central hole in the top. Brush with top of the milk or single cream.

Bake for 30–50 minutes, according to the size of the apples, at gas 6, 200°C (400°F). Alternatively, lower the heat after 20 minutes to gas 4, 180°C (350°F) and allow extra cooking time. Test them with a skewer through the central hole. The apple should be tender. Serve with cream.

You can always make a tart on the dumpling principle. Line a tin with pastry, put in the stuffed apples close together, cover with pastry and bake as above, allowing extra time.

[*Fruit Book*]

APPLE MERINGUE PUDDING

A delicious Sunday pudding.

SERVES 6

60 g (2 oz) butter
1 kg (2 lb) eating apples
  or 875 g (1¾ lb) cookers and 125 g (¼ lb)
  quinces

apricot jam, or cinnamon, or cloves
sugar to taste

Meringue

3 egg whites
175 g (6 oz) sugar
1 heaped teaspoon cornflour
1 teaspoon vinegar
60 g (2 oz) blanched and split almonds

Melt the butter in a large pan, and add the apples (and quinces) washed and cut into rough quarters. Cover and simmer gently until there is about an inch of juice in the pan, then turn up the heat until the apples are cooked. They won't burn if the heat is low enough to start with: water is to be avoided. Push the fruit through a sieve and season with sugar and apricot jam (Golden Delicious), or cinnamon or cloves (cookers). Cox's Orange Pippins have a good enough flavour to be left alone usually. With cookers, quince provides the best flavouring of all. Spread the purée into a shallow serving dish, ovenproof, and leave to cool.

To make the meringue, beat the egg whites stiff. Fold in sugar and cornflour, sifted together, and last of all the vinegar. Pile up on top of the apple, keeping the meringue thin at the edges as it will spread a little while cooking. Stick the almonds all over the meringue. Bake at gas ½, 130°C (250°F) for 1–1¼ hours. If the meringue could be browner at the end of this time, turn the heat up a little. Remove from the oven, and serve warm or cold with single cream.

[*Good Things*]

QUINCES BAKED IN THE FRENCH STYLE

Coings au Four

Allow one for each person. Peel and hollow out the cores of six to eight quinces, being careful not to pierce through the bottom of the fruit. Sprinkle each one with lemon juice as you go. Stand the quinces in a buttered gratin dish.

Mix together to a cream 150 g (5 oz) caster sugar, 100 g (3½ oz) lightly salted or unsalted butter, and 3 generous tablespoons of whipping or double cream. Stuff the quinces with this mixture – if there is some left, add halfway through the cooking. Top each quince with a level tablespoon of sugar and bake at gas 5, 190°C (375°F) until the quinces are tender. Serve with cream and sugar.

NOTE Baked quince was Sir Isaac Newton's favourite pudding.

[*Fruit Book*]

HONEYCOMB MOULD

This delicious pudding of childhood should not be relegated to the nursery. Its clear, true flavour (not to be found in packet-mix versions) is a luxury these days. The mixture plops into a jelly mould – choose one with an elaborate pattern – and several hours later it comes out as an elegant three-layered pudding.

SERVES 6

juice and rind of 2 lemons
3 large eggs
15 g (½ oz) gelatine (one packet)
90 g (3 oz) sugar
500 ml (¾ pt) Channel Islands milk
6 tablespoons cream

Separate the yolks and whites of the eggs. Put the yolks in a large basin. Add the thinly pared lemon rind, gelatine, sugar and cream. Heat the milk to just under boiling point and whisk into the egg yolk mixture (creamy Channel Islands milk, gold top milk, gives the best results). Set the basin over a pan of simmering water, and stir until you have a custard the consistency of double cream more or less.

Taste and add more sugar if you like, but this pudding should not be very sweet. Mix in the lemon juice and strain the custard into the whites, which should have been stiffly beaten; use a metal rather than a wooden spoon to fold it in. Pour into a 2-pint jelly mould.

When it's firmly set, slip a knife round the edge of the pudding, which will then turn out easily (no need to dip the mould into hot water). It will have a cap of clear lemon jelly, then a thin band of opaque cream jelly, and a honey-combed spongey base which makes a slight crinkling noise as it's eaten.

[*Good Things*]

LEMON SOUFFLÉ

As we're not Christmas pudding eaters, finding it too bulky, too unrefreshing after the turkey course, we've made our own tradition of this cold lemon soufflé. I've tried to vary the recipe by adding orange juice and peel, by altering the amount of eggs and cream, but it's no good. Everyone says, 'Yes, this is nice, but please next year may we have our proper lemon soufflé again?'

SERVES 6–8

4 egg yolks and 4 egg whites
175 g (6 oz) caster sugar
2 large or 3 small lemons

300 ml (½ pt) double cream, or 150 ml (¼ pt)
    each double and single
15 g (½ oz) gelatine (one packet)
60 ml (2 fl oz) hot water
60 g (2 oz) almonds, blanched and split

Put yolks, sugar, grated rind and juice of the lemons into a large pudding basin. Stand it over a pan of simmering water and whisk with a rotary beater until the mixture is a thick liquid, about 5 minutes. Take the pudding basin from the pan, stand it on a table and beat for another 5 minutes. By now it will be pale yellow, and thick and billowy. Dissolve the gelatine in the hot water, and add it to the lemon custard. Whisk the cream until it begins to hold its shape and fold that into the custard. Last of all whisk the egg whites until they are very stiff. Fold in the cream and custard mixture with light movements until everything is amalgamated.

Pour into a collared soufflé dish, and leave in the refrigerator to set. Toast the split almonds in the oven until they're golden brown. When cool, use them to decorate the soufflé. Remove the paper collar before serving, so that the cold soufflé rising above its dish, has the appearance of a well-risen hot soufflé. Single cream may be served with it.

[*Good Things*]

A pudding which deserves its name for the perfect combination of flavours and textures, a most subtle and lovely way to end a meal.

SERVES 4–6

150 g (5 oz) fresh brown or white breadcrumbs
1 heaped tablespoon vanilla sugar
grated rind of 1 large lemon
600 ml (1 pt) milk
60 g (2 oz) lightly salted butter
4 large egg yolks
2 tablespoons blackcurrant jelly, or raspberry jelly
4 large egg whites
125 g (4 oz) caster sugar, plus 1 extra teaspoonful

Put breadcrumbs, vanilla sugar and lemon rind into a pudding basin. Bring the milk and butter to just below boiling point and stir it into the crumbs. Leave for 10 minutes, then beat in the egg yolks thoroughly.

Grease a shallow dish which holds about 1½ litres (2½ pt) with a buttery paper, and pour in the breadcrumb custard. Bake at gas 4, 180°C (350°F) for 30 minutes, or a little less, until just firm – the time will depend on the depth of the dish, and remember that the custard will continue to cook a little in its own heat so that if the centre looks runny underneath the skin do not feel anxious.

Warm the jelly (if you use jam, warm it and sieve it) and spread it over the custard without breaking the surface. Whisk the whites until stiff, mix in half the caster sugar, then whisk again until slightly satiny. With a metal spoon, fold in the rest of the 125 g (4 oz) of sugar. Pile on to the pudding, sprinkle with the extra teaspoonful of sugar and return to the oven for 15 minutes until the meringue is slightly browned and crisp. Serve hot with plenty of cream.

[*English Food*]

EMPEROR'S PANCAKE

Kaiserschmarrn

A fluffy pancake inspired by Emperor Franz Joseph I, and a great Viennese speciality. If you prefer, you can bake the pancake in the oven at gas 6, 200°C (400°F).

SERVES 4

200 g (7 oz) flour
a pinch of salt
60 g (2 oz) caster sugar
4 large egg yolks

3 tablespoons butter, melted
60 g (2 oz) sultanas
scant 500 ml (good ¾ pt) milk
4 large egg whites
a little butter
extra caster sugar

Mix the first six ingredients, then beat in the milk. Whisk the whites stiffly and fold them in. Melt butter in two pans. Divide the mixture between them – it should be about 2 cm (¾ inch) thick. When golden brown, turn and cook on the other side. Pull apart with two forks in the pan, making rough little pieces, and cook briefly, turning them about. Divide between four hot plates and sprinkle with sugar. Serve immediately with *Zwetschkenröster*:

1 kg (2 lb) Zwetschke (Quetsche) plums, or other
    dark plums
150 g (5 oz) sugar
2 cloves
a small cinnamon stick
juice and rind of a lemon

Zwetschke plums can be gently torn apart and the stone picked out, other varieties may need more effort. Simmer remaining ingredients with 125 ml (4 fl oz) water for 5 minutes, then put in the plum halves and stir until thick. The plums should fall into lumpy pieces, the final result 15 being somewhere between a compote and a jam. This mixture can be used for fruit dumplings, too.

Do not give up hope of finding Zwetschke plums in England. I heard of some in Cambridge market recently and the friend who bought them wrote to me that 'Austrians do not think of it as just another plum – like Kraut (smooth cabbage) and Kohl (crinkly cabbage), there is the Pflaume (plum) and the Zwetschke.'

[*European Cookery*]

STRAWBERRY BRULÉE

Adapted from an American recipe, strawberry brulée sounds complicated, but it's really worth the trouble. You need a round, sightly, ovenproof dish (Pyrex is ideal) at least 1 inch deep and about 8½ inches across.

SERVES 6

Sweet shortcrust

250 g (8 oz) flour
2 tablespoons icing sugar
125 g (4 oz) butter
1 egg

Filling

300 ml (½ pt) single cream
150 ml (¼ pt) double cream
3 egg yolks
15–20 large strawberries
1 tablespoon each orange liqueur and sugar
extra caster sugar

Make the pastry in the usual way and line the Pyrex dish. Prick all over with a fork, and bake blind until light brown and cooked. A sheet of foil and haricot beans may be used as well to keep the pastry from rising, but the fork treatment is usually enough.

Boil the cream, both kinds together, for one minute exactly. Stir into the egg yolks, beating with a fork. Set over a pan of simmering water for five minutes, stirring all the time to avoid lumps. Pour through a sieve into a clean basin and leave to cool.

Meanwhile halve the strawberries. Sprinkle with sugar and liqueur and set aside for an hour.

Assemble the tart about 2½ hours before the meal. Arrange the strawberries in a single close layer, flat side down on the pastry case. Mix their juice into the custard and pour over the fruit. Chill for 2 hours. Sprinkle the top with a bare ¼-inch layer of caster sugar. Set under a hot grill, turning from time to time, so that the sugar melts into an even golden-brown marbled sheet of caramel. Chill for

17

half an hour (while serving and eating the first course or courses).

[*Good Things*]

SUMMER PUDDING

This pudding can be made successfully with frozen black-currants – though it seems a shame. One family I know always has it on Christmas Day, after the turkey, as a reminder that summer will come.

SERVES 8–10

> *1 kg (2 lb) blackcurrants, or raspberries, or a*
> *mixture of raspberries, redcurrants and*
> *blackberries*
> *175 g (6 oz) caster sugar*
> *good quality white bread, 1 day old*

Put the fruit and sugar into a bowl, and leave overnight. Next day tip the contents of the bowl into a pan, bring to the boil and simmer gently for 2–3 minutes to cook the fruit lightly. It should make a fair amount of juice.

Cut the bread into slices 1 cm (¼ inch) thick. Remove the crusts. Make a circle from 1 slice to fit the base of a 1½-litre (2½-pt) pudding basin or other bowl. Then cut wedges of bread to fit round the sides. There should be no gaps, so if the wedges do not quite fit together, push in small bits of bread. Pour in half the fruit and juice, put in a slice of bread, then add the rest of the fruit and juice.

Cover the top with one or two layers of bread, trimming off the wedges to make a nice neat finish. Put a plate on top, with a couple of tins to weight the whole thing down, and leave overnight – or for several days if you like – in the refrigerator. (If the bread is not thoroughly impregnated with the brilliant fruit juices, boil up a few more blackcurrants or raspberries and strain the liquor over the white bits which will occur at the top of the pudding.)

Run a thin knife round between the pudding and the basin, put a serving dish upside down on top, and turn the whole thing over quickly. Remove the basin and serve with a great deal of cream; cream is essential for this very strong-flavoured pudding, which because of its flavour goes a long way and should be served in small slices.

[*English Food*]

REDCURRANT CAKE

Ribiselkuchen

The best of redcurrant desserts, and this is an Austrian speciality in the version given to me by a friend who lived many years in Vienna. She makes it now for her dinner parties in Paris, cutting it into smallish squares. The combination of almond pastry, soft and crisp meringue, and sharp red freshness, makes it the ideal end to a meal.

SERVES 6–8

160 g (5 oz) butter
375 g (12 oz) caster sugar
4 egg yolks
100 g (3 oz) ground almonds
300 g (9 oz) flour
500 g (1 lb) redcurrants, free of stalks
4 egg whites

Cream butter and one-third of the sugar, add yolks, almonds and flour. Or else mix to a dough in the processor. Roll out into a circle to fit a 23 cm (9 inch) tart tin, preferably one with a removable base. Bake at gas 5–6, 190–200°C (375–400°F) for 30 minutes or until cooked.

Meanwhile mix redcurrants with half the remaining caster sugar (some people like to cook them gently, then strain off and reduce the liquor, to make a jammy mixture, but this is not necessary except in wet summers). Whip egg whites until stiff, again add half remaining sugar and whip once more until thick and soft. Finally fold in the last of the sugar.

Take the almond base from the oven. Raise the heat to gas 7, 220°C (425°F). Spread redcurrants, and sugar (or their thick syrup) over the pastry, leaving a narrow rim of cake free. Pile on the meringue, right to the edge of the cake. Fork it up and put into the oven for 15–20 minutes until the meringue is nicely caught with brown. Be guided entirely by appearance, rather than precise timing. Serve warm or cold.

NOTE If you want to get ahead, make the whole thing earlier in the day. Or just make the base the day before and complete with redcurrants and meringue nearer the time of serving.

You can use other sharp fruit, raspberries, gooseberries – use young green ones and cook them first – or in winter a pureé of dried apricots cooked in orange juice.

GOOSEBERRY FOOL

Too often gooseberries are overcooked, then sieved or liquidized to a smooth slop. Ideally, they should be very lightly cooked, then crushed with a fork, before being folded into whipped cream. Egg custard is an honourable, and an ancient alternative to cream; commercial powder custard is not. Don't spoil this springtime luxury. It's better to halve the quantities, than to serve a great floury bowlful.

SERVES 4–6

375 g (12 oz) young gooseberries, topped and tailed
60 g (2 oz) butter

> sugar
>
> 300 ml (½ pt) double cream, whipped,
> or 150 ml (¼ pt) each double and single cream
> or 300 ml (½ pt) single cream and 3 egg yolks

Stew the gooseberries slowly in a covered pan, with the butter, until they are yellow and just cooked. Crush with a fork, sweeten to taste and mix them carefully and lightly into the whipped cream.

To make the custard, bring single cream (or rich milk) to the boil, and pour on to the egg yolks, whisking all the time. Set the bowl over a pan of hot water and stir steadily until the custard thickens to double cream consistency. Strain into a bowl, and leave to cool before folding in the gooseberries.

Serve in custard glasses or plain white cups, with some homemade almond biscuits or macaroons.

Gooseberry fools can be frozen and served as cream ice: in this case, sieve the fruit as the pieces of gooseberry produced by mashing would spoil the texture of the ice. Later in the year other fruit may be substituted for gooseberries, uncooked raspberries and strawberries and peaches for instance, and in the autumn cooked purées of apple flavoured with apricot jam, and of quinces. Use just over half a pint of purée to half a pint of cream or custard.

[*Good Things*]

DUCLAIR CHERRY TART

Tarte aux Cerises de Duclair

Duclair is on the Seine upstream from Tancarville, not far from Rouen. Ducks are a speciality, so is this unusual cherry tart. The tricky bit is cooking the cherries so that they caramelize without becoming overcooked: you need a high heat once the butter, sugar and Calvados are blended, but take care the cherry juices do not burn – this kind of thing is much easier to do on a gas burner than an electric ring.

You need a puff pastry case, baked blind in a 23–25-cm (9–10-inch) tart tin. This can be done in advance, and the case reheated to freshen it if necessary. The cream and cheese can also be mixed earlier in the day. But the cooking of the cherries and the final assembly should take place not too long before the meal.

SERVES 6–8

500 g (1 lb) firm red cherries, stoned weight
60 g (2 oz) butter
100 g (3½ oz) granulated sugar
3 tablespoons Calvados or malt whisky
250 g (8 oz) fromage frais
caster sugar
150 ml (¼ pt) double cream

Drain the cherries in a sieve. Melt the butter, stir in the granulated sugar and Calvados, or whisky. When they are blended, raise the heat and put in the cherries. They should caramelize lightly, so keep them moving and do not take your eye off them. Drain and cool.

Beat the *fromage frais* with caster sugar to taste. Whip the cream and fold it in, check again for sweetness and taste a cherry to make sure that you do not over-sweeten the mixture.

To assemble, spread the cream cheese and cream on to the pastry. Put the cherries on top.

[*Fruit Book*]

BILBERRY TART FROM ALSACE

Tarte aux Myrtilles

SERVES 6

The Vosges mountains, like the Massif Central, are much visited in August and September by families on a Sunday search for bilberries. When they get home and pick the fruit over, they are often disappointed at the tiny quantity. As we are likely to be, picking by hand in the Lake District or Derbyshire.

24   The thing to do is to find a tart tin into which the bil-

berries you have picked fit in a nice close thick layer, coming a third of the way up the tin. Then tip them back into their bowl.

Line the tin with sweet shortcrust pastry. Scatter the base with bread, biscuit or cake crumbs thinly. Then put in the fruit. Bake for 15 minutes at gas 6–7, 200–220°C (400–425°F).

Meanwhile, for about 500 g (1 lb) bilberries, beat up together 150 ml (¼ pt) whipping cream, 100 g (3½ oz) sugar and 2 egg yolks. Pour over the bilberries and return to the oven until the cream is set – 10 to 15 minutes.

NOTE If your quantity is particularly small, make tartlets, and reduce the cream ingredients by half.

[*Fruit Book*]

PRUNE TART

A dish from Tours. For success, the prune purée must be rich and well-flavoured, not in the least watery.

SERVES 6

250 g (8 oz) shortcrust pastry
500 g (1 lb) giant prunes, soaked
sugar
water

rum
beaten egg

Line a tart tin with a removable base with pastry (save the trimmings). Prick all over with a fork and bake blind until cooked, but not very brown.

Simmer the prunes in just enough water to cover them. Drain and sieve. Flavour the purée with sugar and rum, and put into the pastry case. Using the pastry trimmings, make a criss-cross lattice over it, with strips about ¼ inch wide. Brush the pastry with beaten egg, and bake until golden brown. Serve with cream.

NOTE Mix the prune purée above with double its weight in homemade vanilla ice-cream. Refreeze. Serve with almond biscuits. I know this sounds unpromising, but try it.

[*Good Things*]

PLUM AND WALNUT PIE

A most delicious pie, with walnuts, cinnamon and butter to counteract the fruit's acidity. Choose a mild plum: the Quetsche or Zwetschken is ideal.

SERVES 6

shortcrust pastry
500 g (1 lb) plums, halved, stoned, chopped

125 g (4 oz) soft light brown or demerara sugar
125 g (4 oz) chopped walnuts
2 teaspoons ground cinnamon
grated rind of ½ lemon and ½ orange
60 g (2 oz) melted butter
beaten egg or top of the milk to glaze

Line a 20–23-cm (8–9-inch) pie dish about 2.5-cm (1-inch)
deep with pastry. Mix plums, sugar, walnuts, cinnamon and
grated rinds and put into the pastry. Pour over the butter.
Cover with pastry, pinching the edges and making a central
hole. Brush over with beaten egg or top of the milk. Bake
at gas 5, 190°C (375°F) for about an hour. Serve warm
rather than hot with cream.

This pie can also be made with greengages, almonds and
white sugar.

[*Fruit Book*]

SPRINGFIELD PEAR CAKE

Every autumn, our fruit-farming neighbour at Springfield
gives his friends the fine large almost-ripe pears that he
cannot sell to the shops because they have slight blemishes.
This is a favourite way of using them, to make an upside-
down cake flavoured with ginger.

Top

90 g *(3 oz) lightly-salted Danish butter, cut up*
90 g *(3 oz) granulated sugar*
2 tablespoons syrup from preserved ginger
3 or 4 large firm pears
juice of a lemon

Cake

125 g *(4 oz) softened butter*
125 g *(4 oz) caster sugar*
100 g *(3½ oz) self-raising flour*
1 level teaspoon baking powder
30 g *(1 oz) ground almonds*
2 large eggs
3–4 tablespoons syrup from preserved ginger
4 knobs preserved ginger, coarsely chopped

Take a shallow cake tin or *moule à manquer* that measures 23–25 cm (9½–10 inch) across and at least 3½ cm (1¼ inches) deep. Set it over a low heat and put in the Danish butter. Stir about with a wooden spoon, pushing the butter up the sides of the tin to grease them. Add sugar and syrup and stir about until you have a rich creamy-fawn bubbling mixture, a pale toffee mixture. Remove from the heat.

28   Peel, core and thinly slice the pears, turning them in

lemon juice on a plate so that they do not discolour. Arrange them in a sunflower effect on the toffee base. Put the larger pieces round the outside, curved side down and overlapping, so that the base is evenly covered with two rings of pear slices, and some central pieces.

Tip all the cake ingredients, except the chopped ginger, into an electric mixer bowl or processor, and whizz to smoothness. Or beat everything vigorously together with a wooden spoon. Add the ginger and spread over the top of the pears. Bake at gas 5, 190°C (375°F) for 45 minutes. If the top is richly brown and well risen, turn the heat down to gas 4, 180°C (350°F). Leave another 15 minutes, or until the edges of the cake have slightly contracted from the tin, and a skewer pushed in almost horizontally comes out clean. Leave to cool for a few minutes on a wire rack, then run a broad knife blade between the tin and the edge of the cake to make sure there are no sticking patches.

Put a serving plate with a rim on top, upside-down, then turn the whole thing as rapidly as possible – use a cloth to protect your hands. A certain amount of juice will flow from the cake, but this only adds to its deliciousness.

Serve hot, warm or cold, on its own, or with cream as a pudding. It's a spoon-and-fork cake, being far too messy to eat with your fingers at afternoon tea.

[*Fruit Book*]

The best of all English boiled suet puddings. In the middle the butter and sugar melt to a rich sauce, which is sharpened with the juice from the lemon. The genius of the pudding is the lemon. Its citrus bitter flavour is a subtlety which raises the pudding to the highest class. When you serve it, make sure that everyone has a piece of the lemon, which will be much softened by the cooking, but still vigorous.

Once when I had no lemons, I used a couple of small limes, which were equally successful.

The name of the pudding refers to the sauce, which runs out of it when it is turned on to a serving dish, and provides it with a moat of buttery brown liquid.

SERVES 4–6

250 g (8 oz) self-raising flour
125 g (4 oz) chopped fresh beef suet
milk and water
slightly salted butter
soft light brown or caster sugar
1 large lemon, or 2 limes

Mix the flour and suet together in a bowl. Make into a
30   dough with milk and water, half and half; about 150 ml

(¼ pt). The dough should be soft, but not too soft to roll out into a large circle. Cut a quarter out of this circle, to be used later as the lid of the pudding.

Butter a pudding basin lavishly. It should hold about 1½ litres (2½ pints). Drop the three-quarter-circle of pastry into it, and press the cut sides together to make a perfect join. Put about 100 g (3⅓ oz) each of butter, cut up, and sugar into the pastry. Prick the lemon (or limes) all over with a larding needle, so that the juices will be able to escape, then put it on to the butter and sugar. Fill the rest of the cavity with equal weights of sugar and butter cut in pieces – at least another 100 g, possibly more.

Roll out the pastry that was set aside to make a lid. Lay it on top of the filling, and press the edges together so that the pudding is sealed in completely.

Put a piece of foil right over the basin, with a pleat in the middle. Tie it in place with string, and make a string handle over the top so that the pudding can be lifted about easily. Put a large pan of water on to boil, and lower the pudding into it; the water must be boiling, and it should come halfway, or a little further, up the basin. Cover and leave to boil for 3–4 hours. If the water gets low, replenish it with *boiling* water.

To serve, put a deep dish over the basin after removing the foil lid, and quickly turn the whole thing upside down: it is a good idea to ease the pudding from the sides of the basin with a knife first. Put on the table immediately.

[*English Food*] 31

APRICOT AND ALMOND CRUMBLE

An elegant version of the homely crumble. It is always a great success with our French and Italian friends, who ask for an English pudding but whose pioneering spirit would fail if faced with Spotted Dick or Dead Man's Leg.

SERVES 6

24 large apricots
sugar
60 g (2 oz) blanched, slivered almonds

Crumble

125 g (4 oz) flour
125 g (4 oz) caster sugar
125 g (4 oz) ground almonds
175 g (6 oz) butter

Peel and quarter apricots (if the skins are in good condition and not tough, you need not bother with the peeling). Arrange them in a shallow baking dish. Sprinkle with sugar. Mix dry crumble ingredients together, then rub in butter. Spread over fruit. Top with the slivered almonds. Bake at gas 6, 200°C (400°F) until the top is nicely coloured – about 35 minutes. If you find the top colouring too rapidly, lower the heat to gas 4, 180°C (350°F).

Serve hot or warm, with cream or custard sauce.

[English Food]

GRILLED PEACHES

Cut the peaches (one per person) in half and remove the stones. Brush the cut sides with butter and sprinkle with sugar generously. Grill cut-side up, gently at first to heat the peaches through, then more fiercely to brown the sugar. Serve hot with vanilla ice cream, or with whipped cream.

[Fruit Book]

BANANAS WITH APRICOT SAUCE

The simplest of all banana recipes – if you have on a hot or moderate oven, you can bake the bananas until they are soft instead of boiling them. If you are lucky enough to find small Canary bananas, buy two per person. One of the giant-sized kind that you usually see is enough for most people at the end of a meal.

4–8 bananas, left unpeeled
250 g (8 oz) apricot jam
4 tablespoons water
apricot brandy or orange liqueur to taste

Make the sauce first, and keep it warm. Simmer jam and water until smoothly amalgamated. Sieve it into a sauceboat and stir in the brandy or liqueur to taste. Keep the sauceboat warm in a water bath.

Bring a large pan, half full of water, to the boil. Put in the unpeeled bananas and boil for four minutes (just like boiling an egg).

To eat the bananas, each person peels away a strip of skin and opens it out a little – the most delicious smell rises with the steam – to make room for some apricot sauce.

[*Fruit Book*]

BANANA TRIFLE

No more than a normal trifle with a layer of bananas through the middle, but it has been a particular favourite at Christmas parties for many years. In summertime, you might substitute cherries, strawberries or raspberries for the bananas, or lightly cooked peach or apricot slices.

When you measure the ingredients, have extra cake or macaroons in reserve. Your large glass bowl may be bigger or squarer than mine, and need odd corners filling in. There is no reason, for instance, why you should not use both macaroons and cake, or slices of home-made sponge roll with apricot or any other appropriate jam in it. Again, wine can be what you have – we usually bring a small store of

Muscat de Frontignan back from France that we save up
for Christmas, but other muscat wines can be used instead,
or Sauternes.

SERVES 6–8

6 large macaroons or pound of sponge cake slices
kirsch or apricot brandy or fruit eau de vie of an
    appropriate kind
sweet dessert wine
500 ml (¾ pt) single cream
half a vanilla pod, split
2 large eggs
2 large egg yolks
caster sugar from vanilla pod jar
strawberry, raspberry or apricot jam
2–3 ripe, firm bananas
pared rind and juice of a lemon
300 ml (½ pt) double cream
pinch nutmeg
toasted almonds and candied peel for decoration

Make a ground-floor layer of macaroons or cake in the
bottom of a large glass bowl. Pour over it 3 tablespoons of
whichever spirit you use, and 150 ml (¼ pt) wine. Give this
a chance to soak in, then add more wine if you think the
macaroons or cake are on the dry side.

Make the custard by boiling the single cream with the

35

vanilla pod. Beat egg and yolks together; pour on the boiling cream, whisking, then return to pan and stir over a low heat until thickened. Sweeten to taste. Cool, remove the vanilla pod.

While the custard cools, spread a layer of jam over the sponge cake or macaroon layer. Then slice the bananas – after peeling them, of course – and arrange the pieces closely together on top.

Spoon the cooled custard carefully over the banana, starting with the outside, then moving in. This prevents the banana slices being dislodged.

At this stage, it is a good idea to leave the trifle in the refrigerator overnight, for everything to bed down together.

At the same time, put the lemon rind and juice in a bowl with 2 tablespoons of whichever spirit you used, and 8 tablespoons of the wine. Next day, strain the juice into a large bowl, and stir in 60 g (2 oz) caster sugar. Still stirring, pour in the cream slowly, and add the nutmeg. Beat with a whisk until the syllabub holds its shape – do not overbeat or the cream will curdle.

Pile on to the trifle, either right across or in a circle round the edge. Decorate with almonds and peel, or whatever else you like to use. At Christmas, people seem to go wild with glacé cherries, and angelica, in emulation of holly I suppose, but quieter decorations are more appropriate to a real trifle of this kind, made with the best of everything.

[*Fruit Book*]

Here is a simple way of baking figs that are ripe and soft, whole, but on the verge of splitting. Use figs of a kind that do not need peeling and select approximately two per person.

First find an ovenproof dish that can be set on the table afterwards. A plain brown terrine is ideal, better than a gratin dish, as the higher sides give the figs support and prevent the juices burning. It should just hold the figs, stalk end up, close together.

Remove the figs, dip them one by one in water and roll them in caster sugar from the vanilla jar, so that they are quite snow-covered. Put them straight into the dish, as you finish each one.

Bake them in a hot oven, gas 7–8, 220–230°C (425–450°F) for about 20 minutes, but check after 12 minutes. They are done when the sugar has disappeared and turned into a rich brown juice at the bottom of the dish.

Cool, then chill thoroughly. Serve them with cream if you like, and sugar or lemon thins or almond biscuits.

[*Fruit Book*]

LIGHT BLUEBERRY CHEESECAKE

Finding many cheesecakes too cloying on account of the full-fat soft cheese they are made with, I now make a light version with *fromage frais*. If you cannot buy it, make a fuss – it really is the best of the soft cheeses to use with fruit, the fat content is medium (in the brand we import anyway), the consistency just right.

Macaroons can also be a problem. People in the bakery trade assure me that no ground rice is used in commercial macaroons. What therefore makes them taste so nasty? I suspect that synthetic almond essence – or 'flavouring' – is added to the mix that bakers buy from their wholesalers. To get round the problem, I buy French packet macaroons, but this is expensive. Sometimes shortbread or other crisp biscuits are used instead.

Line a tart tin of 20 cm (8 inches) with sweet shortcrust pastry. Assemble the following:

SERVES 6

150–175 g (5–6 oz) blueberries
50 g (1½ oz) caster sugar
60 g (2 oz) macaroons, crushed
250 g (8 oz) fromage frais
2 good tablespoons cream, whipping or double

2 large egg yolks
about a tablespoon granulated sugar
1 large egg white, whisked

Mix blueberries with the sugar. Sprinkle a generous half of the macaroon crumbs over the pastry and put the blueberry mixture on top. Beat the *fromage frais* with the cream and yolks, then put in the sugar. Taste and add a little more if you like, but do not oversweeten. Fold in the egg white. Spread on top of the fruit and sprinkle with the remaining macaroon crumbs.

Bake at gas 7, 220°C (425°F) for 15 minutes, then at gas 4, 180°C (350°F) for half an hour longer, or until the filling is puffed up and just set. It will sink as it cools and become firmer.

[*Fruit Book*]

RICE PUDDING

Anyone who feels an aversion to rice puddings, may be encouraged to try this one and think again.

SERVES 6

125 g (4 oz) long grain rice
600 ml (1 pt) milk
½ a vanilla pod

4 egg yolks
125 g (4 oz) sugar
2 heaped teaspoons gelatine
300 ml (½ pt) double cream

Boil the rice in water for 3 minutes, then drain and rinse it under the cold tap. Return to the pan with half the milk, cover and simmer until very tender. Bring the rest of the milk to the boil with the vanilla pod, then whisk into the yolks and the sugar. Pour back into the pan and stir over a lowish heat until the custard thickens (use a double boiler if you are not accustomed to making egg custards). Melt the gelatine in 2 tablespoons of hot water and add to the hot custard. Strain into a bowl, and add the cooked rice which will have absorbed all the milk. Cool. Whip cream and fold in. Turn into a lightly oiled mould. Chill, and serve with soft fruit or stewed pears that have been lightly poached in syrup.

[*Food with the Famous*]

CRÈME BRULÉE AUX KIWIS

Burnt cream has been made in England since the seventeenth century, but it gained a new reputation when a chef at Trinity College, Cambridge, took it up at the end of the last century. Being a rich pudding, it was usually served with fruit. Not long ago, someone had the idea of putting grapes underneath the pudding. And why not? Kiwi fruit taste even better than grapes, so do Sharon persimmons which can be cut into slices and eaten while they are still firm (unlike other persimmons which have to be very soft). Raspberries and poached sliced peaches and pears do well, too.

The success of burnt cream depends partly on the flavour of the cream you use. Loseley or other farm brands or *crème fraîche* are ideal. Indeed, if you can buy one of them, and are in a hurry, you can use it whipped, instead of making a custard.

SERVES 10−12

about 750 g (1½ lb) Kiwi fruit
1 litre (1¾ pt) cream
thinly cut peel of a lemon
5-cm (2-inch) cinnamon stick
4 large eggs
4 large egg yolks
sugar

Choose a large gratin dish that will hold 1½ litres (2½ pt) at least. Cover the base with peeled and sliced kiwis.

Bring cream, peel and cinnamon slowly to just under boiling point. Strain on to eggs and yolks that have been beaten together in a large pudding basin: whisk together 41 vigorously at first, then occasionally until you have a smooth cream. Put the basin over a pan of barely simmering water, and stir with a wooden spoon until very thick – the back of the spoon should be coated. Should the custard begin to show a hint of graininess, rapidly pour it into a processor or liquidizer and whizz at top speed for a few minutes. Pour over the fruit and chill for several hours.

A couple of hours before serving, sprinkle enough granulated sugar over the whole thing to make a ½-centimetre (scant ¼-inch) depth. Preheat the grill to make it as red as possible. Slip the dish underneath. Do not turn your back on it, but be patient and watch as the sugar melts to a marbled brown glassiness. If the grill heat is uneven, you will have to turn the dish.

Some people stand the gratin dish in a tray of crushed ice before grilling the sugar. This is a good idea if your grill is not very hot, as it prevents the custard overheating underneath and bubbling up through the sugar. But I have never found it necessary.

The quantities above make enough for ten or even a dozen people, depending on the rest of the meal.

[*Fruit Book*]

CREAM CHEESE MOUSSE

A simple delicious mousse, one of the delights of summer when served with strawberries (or other soft fruit, but particularly strawberries). It's really a more elaborate form of *coeur à la crème*, made with the low-fat cheese on sale in most grocer's shops.

SERVES 6

250 g (8 oz) low-fat cottage cheese
2 egg yolks
60 g (2 oz) sugar, vanilla sugar for preference
15 g (½ oz) gelatine (one packet)
6 tablespoons very hot water
125 g (4 oz) each double and single cream

Sieve the cottage cheese to get rid of the large-grained texture (if homemade cheese is used, make sure it's well drained before weighing.) Beat in egg yolks and sugar.

Dissolve the gelatine in the hot water, add the two creams and whisk until stiff. Fold in the cheese carefully, so that the mixture is well blended, but still light and fluffy. Brush a 1½-pint mould (or little heart-shaped moulds) with a thin film of non-tasting oil and sprinkle with caster sugar. Pour in the mousse and leave to set.

Serve chilled, with unchilled strawberries dressed with a little orange juice or orange liqueur.

[*Good Things*]

PARIS–BREST

SERVES 6–8

choux pastry made with 125 g (4 oz) flour
60g (2 oz) blanched almonds
300 ml (½ pt) cream, whipped
*   or 250 g (8 oz) butter cream*
125 g (4 oz) praline powder (see below)
icing sugar

Pipe the choux paste into a circle on a greased baking tray, a circle about the size of a dinner plate. Sprinkle the top with split and slivered almonds – the pieces should not be too small. Bake for 20 minutes in a hot oven (gas 7, 220°C, 425°F), 10 minutes at gas 4, 180°C (350°F). Slice across into two while hot, and leave to cool. Just before the meal, sandwich the two pieces together with plenty of whipped cream or butter cream, flavoured with praline powder. Dredge with icing sugar. Like all choux pastry, this cake will not appreciate standing around, or being kept until next day, with the filling in it.

To make praline powder

Put 125 g (4 oz) of unblanched almonds and 125 g (4 oz) sugar into a heavy pan. Stir in 4 tablespoons of water, and heat gently so that the sugar melts. Raise the heat slightly so that the syrup gradually darkens to caramel – stir from time to time. The nuts will pop when they are ready. Have a bowl of very cold water handy and stand the base of the pan into it to prevent the caramel going any darker.

If you want to make praline powder, spread the mixture out on to a greased metal sheet. Leave it to cool and harden, then break it up and reduce to a powder in a blender or processor. Store in a screw-top glass jar.

[*Good Things*]

DEVONSHIRE JUNKET

Not a nursery pudding. Junket is an English version of those curd and cream dishes that the French still make in such delicious variety (*cremets d'Angers, maingaux, coeurs à la crème*). Like their *fromage frais*, junket is produced by curdling warm milk with rennet. Then it is left to set to a smooth jelly. The curd is not broken up and drained of whey as it would be in France, and as it once was in England (junket derives from old Norman French, *jonquet*, a little basket

45

made from *jonques* or rushes and used for draining cheeses until recent times).

When we had the idea of leaving the curd alone in its smoothness, I do not know. In *Food and Drink in Britain*, C. Anne Wilson quotes the earliest recipe she can find, from 1653, in which the junket was not drained, but eaten with cream and cinnamon just as in the recipe below. She suggests that it was the popularity of unrenneted creams in the eighteenth century, the syllabubs, fools, fruit creams, which sent the junket into eclipse. Like many old dishes that have survived at the fringes of the country, it has acquired the reputation of being a local speciality, in this case of Devonshire, which is really unjustified – or perhaps one should rather say misleading. The production of rennet in convenient bottled form – rennet extract was first prepared by a chemist in Denmark in the 1870s and was in production from 1878 onwards – unfortunately meant that junket could become the bane of every nursery, with an ultimate degradation of artificial colouring and flavour. From my own experience, I recall hating the texture of junket as a child. Like apricots and rice pudding, it used to end up in the aspidistra pot which stood so helpfully in the middle of the junior dining-table at school.

SERVES 4 – 6

600 ml (1 pt) Channel Island milk
1 dessertspoon sugar

46

2 tablespoons brandy (optional)
1 teaspoon rennet
150 g (¼ pt) clotted cream
cinnamon or nutmeg

Bring milk slowly to blood heat – if you are not used to judging this, use a thermometer, it is surprising how hot a liquid at 37°C (98.4°F) feels. Meanwhile mix the sugar and brandy in the china bowl in which you intend to serve the junket. And put it in a convenient place in the kitchen, where it can stay until required (junket sets best at room temperature). Pour the warmed milk into the bowl, then stir in the rennet gently. Do not disturb until the junket is firmly set.

If the clotted cream is stiff, mix it with a little fresh cream, so that it can be spread over the surface of the junket without disturbing it. Sprinkle the cream with ground cinnamon or nutmeg.

If the junket tastes salty, your teaspoonful of rennet was too generous.

[*English Food*]

ELIZABETH RAFFALD'S ORANGE CUSTARDS

The majority of the best cookery books in this country have been written by women (or by foreigners). And of this energetic tribe, the most energetic of all was Elizabeth

Raffald. Consider her career. She started work at fifteen, in 1748, ending up as housekeeper at Arley Hall in Cheshire. At thirty she married. Eighteen years later she was dead. During those eighteen years she organized:

(a) a cooked-food shop selling pies, brawn, pickles, etc.;
(b) an enlarged cooked-food shop, with a confectionery department;
(c) the first domestic servants' employment agency;
(d) two important Manchester inns, or rather posting-houses;
(e) the first street and trade directory in Manchester (then a town of something over twenty thousand inhabitants);
(f) a couple of newspapers, as an *eminence rose*;
(g) an unreliable husband;
(h) fifteen (or sixteen – some conflict of evidence) daughters;
(i) her cookery book, *The Experienced English Housekeeper*, published in 1769 (a facsimile of the 8th edition is available from E. & W. Books). Many of her recipes can be adapted to modern kitchen machinery, which she would thoroughly have approved of. She could always see the advantages of the latest thing, and added her own contribution to progress.

SERVES 8 – 10

rind of ½ Seville orange
1 tablespoon brandy (or orange liqueur)

juice of 1 Seville orange
125 g (4 oz) granulated sugar
6 large egg yolks, or extra large for preference
300 ml (½ pt) double cream
300 ml (½ pt) single cream
candied orange peel

The rind can be removed from half the orange with a potato peeler: simmer it in water for 2 minutes, then drain it and place in the blender with the brandy (or liqueur) and the orange juice, sugar and egg yolks. Blend at top speed until the peel is reduced to a very slight grittiness in the liquid. Bring creams to the boil, and add gradually to the mixture in the blender. Check the seasoning, and add more sugar and orange juice if necessary.

Pour into 8 or 10 custard cups or small soufflé dishes. Stand them in a pan of hot water and put into a warm oven, gas 3, 160°C (325°F) until just set – about 30 minutes or a little longer, depending on the depth of the mixture in the pots.

Serve warm or chilled, with a decorative piece of candied orange peel in the centre of each one.

[English Food]

ZABAGLIONE

A foamy Italian pudding or sauce that goes well with such fruit dishes as baked bananas, or lightly-cooked pears. It amounts to a light custard. The problem is that it should really be made between courses so that it can be served immediately. If you have visitors who can relax, or if you are eating in the kitchen anyway, this makes no difficulty.

Quantities for one person are usually as follows – but for a sauce you could reduce quantities by a third:

> *1 large egg yolk*
> *1 rounded tablespoon caster sugar*
> *2 tablespoons Marsala, or other sweet wine*

Put ingredients into a large pudding basin, set it over a pan of barely simmering water which should not touch the bottom of the basin, and whisk steadily with a rotary beater. Or an electric beater, which will halve the time needed.

The mixture will increase bulkily up the bowl, turn pale and take on a rich but light consistency. Serve at this point for a warm sauce or pudding. Continue to whisk for another 5 minutes, then remove from the pan and whisk until cold, if you are serving the zabaglione at a later stage.

As a pudding, it is usually served in glasses.

[*Fruit Book*]

LEMON ICE CREAM

SERVES 6

zest and juice of 6 large lemons
300 g (10 oz) sugar
1 level teaspoon cornflour
4 large egg yolks
250 ml (8 fl oz) whipping cream, whisked until
*   stiff*

Bring zest, juice, 200 ml (7 fl oz) water and sugar slowly to
the boil, stirring to dissolve the sugar. After boiling for a
second or two, fish out the strips of zest (before they make
the syrup bitter) and leave the syrup to boil for 4 minutes.

Put the cornflour and yolks into the bowl of an electric
mixer. Mix until the yolks are thick, and the syrup has come
to the end of its boiling time. Pour the syrup on to the egg
yolks, still being beaten, and go on beating until the mixture
is foamy and smooth. Cool and fold cream into the egg-
lemon mixture. Freeze in the usual way. This mixture does
not need beating half way through freezing.

[*Fruit Book*]

BANANA ICE CREAM

A mild but intriguing ice cream, set off by pieces of almond praline.

SERVES 6

750 g (1½ lb) bananas
juice of a lemon
200 g (7 oz) sugar
1−2 tablespoons white rum or kirsch
500−600 ml (¾−1 pt) double or whipping cream
almond praline (see p. 45)

Peel, break up and process the bananas, or liquidize them, with the lemon juice. Dissolve the sugar in 200 ml (7 fl oz) of water over a low heat, bring to boiling point and boil hard for 3−5 minutes, until there is 300 ml (½ pt) syrup. Add to it 200 ml (7 fl oz) of cold water and add, with the rum or kirsch, to the banana.

Whip the cream until it is very thick but not stiff. Fold into the banana mixture carefully. Freeze in the usual way, with a sorbetière, ice bucket or freezer, following the appropriate instructions.

When you serve the ice cream, scatter it with the praline, broken up into small pieces, not crumbs.

[*Fruit Book*]

WATER-MELON SORBET

SERVES 6

750 g (1½ lb) water-melon pieces, minus seeds
300 g (10 oz) sugar
2 sticks cinnamon
juice of a large lemon

Mash or liquidize or sieve the water-melon to make a smooth pulp. Simmer sugar with ½ litre (¾ pt) water and the cinnamon for 5 minutes. When cool, remove cinnamon, and add the syrup gradually to the water-melon, stopping when the balance of fruit and sweetness seems right. Use the lemon juice to bring out the flavour.

Freeze in the usual way, at the lowest possible temperature. If you can stir the sorbet from time to time, to keep the texture even, you can serve it at the granita stage, when it is a thick grainy sludge. Very cooling.

As they say in Egypt, 'Fill your stomach with a summer water-melon' – in other words, don't worry, relax, enjoy yourself.

[*Fruit Book*]

PENGUIN 60s

PENGUIN 60s

LAURIE LEE · *To War in Spain*

PATRICK LEIGH FERMOR · *Loose as the Wind*

ELMORE LEONARD · *Trouble at Rindo's Station*

DAVID LODGE · *Surprised by Summer*

BERNARD MAC LAVERTY · *The Miraculous Candidate*

SHENA MACKAY · *Cloud-Cuckoo-Land*

NORMAN MAILER · *The Dressing Room*

PETER MAYLE · *Postcards from Summer*

JAN MORRIS · *Scenes from Havian Life*

BLAKE MORRISON · *Camp Cuba*

VLADIMIR NABOKOV · *Now Remember*

REDMOND O'HANLON · *A River in Borneo*

STEVEN PINKER · *Thinking in Tongues*

CRAIG RAINE · *Private View*

CLAUDIA RODEN · *Ful Medames and Other Vegetarian Dishes*

HELGE RUBINSTEIN · *Chocolate Parfait*

SIMON SCHAMA · *The Taking of the Bastille*

WILL SELF · *The Rock of Crack As Big As the Ritz*

MARK SHAND · *Elephant Tales*

NIGEL SLATER · *30-Minute Suppers*

RICK STEIN · *Fresh from the Sea*

LYTTON STRACHEY · *Florence Nightingale*

PAUL THEROUX · *Slow Trains to Simla*

COLIN THUBRON · *Samarkand*

MARK TULLY · *Beyond Purdah*

LAURENS VAN DER POST · *Merry Christmas, Mr Lawrence*

MARGARET VISSER · *More than Meets the Eye*

GAVIN YOUNG · *Something of Samoa*

and

Thirty Obituaries from Wisden · SELECTED BY MATTHEW ENGEL

READ MORE IN PENGUIN

For complete information about books available from Penguin and how to order them, please write to us at the appropriate address below. Please note that for copyright reasons the selection of books varies from country to country.

IN THE UNITED KINGDOM: Please write to *Dept. EP, Penguin Books Ltd, Bath Road, Harmondsworth, Middlesex UB7 0DA.*

IN THE UNITED STATES: Please write to *Consumer Sales, Penguin USA, P.O. Box 999, Dept. 17109, Bergenfield, New Jersey 07621-0120.* VISA and MasterCard holders call 1-800-253-6476 to order Penguin titles.

IN CANADA: Please write to *Penguin Books Canada Ltd, 10 Alcorn Avenue, Suite 300, Toronto, Ontario M4V 3B2.*

IN AUSTRALIA: Please write to *Penguin Books Australia Ltd, P.O. Box 257, Ringwood, Victoria 3134.*

IN NEW ZEALAND: Please write to *Penguin Books (NZ) Ltd, Private Bag 102902, North Shore Mail Centre, Auckland 10.*

IN INDIA: Please write to *Penguin Books India Pvt Ltd, 706 Eros Apartments, 56 Nehru Place, New Delhi 110 019.*

IN THE NETHERLANDS: Please write to *Penguin Books Netherlands bv, Postbus 3507, NL-1001 AH Amsterdam.*

IN GERMANY: Please write to *Penguin Books Deutschland GmbH, Metzlerstrasse 26, 60594 Frankfurt am Main.*

IN SPAIN: Please write to *Penguin Books S. A., Bravo Murillo 19, 1° B, 28015 Madrid.*

IN ITALY: Please write to *Penguin Italia s.r.l., Via Felice Casati 20, I-20124 Milano.*

IN FRANCE: Please write to *Penguin France S. A., 17 rue Lejeune, F-31000 Toulouse.*

IN JAPAN: Please write to *Penguin Books Japan, Ishikiribashi Building, 2-5-4, Suido, Bunkyo-ku, Tokyo 112.*

IN GREECE: Please write to *Penguin Hellas Ltd, Dimocritou 3, GR-106 71 Athens.*

IN SOUTH AFRICA: Please write to *Longman Penguin Southern Africa (Pty) Ltd, Private Bag X08, Bertsham 2013.*